LAUREN WINDLE

DRAWING AS PRAYER

Connect with God through the Bible and sketching

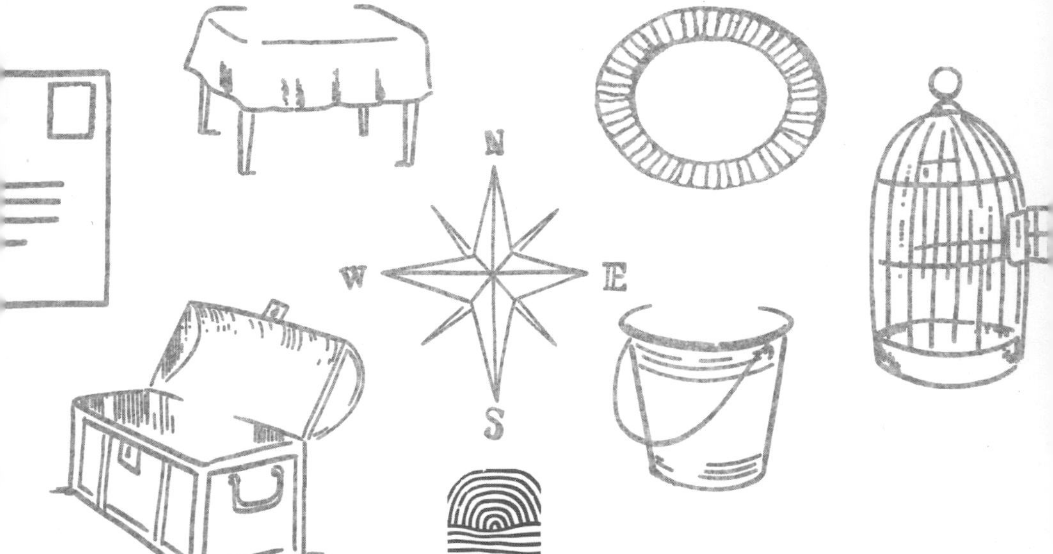

N

W

E

S

FORM

First published in Great Britain in 2025

Form
Part of the SPCK Group
Studio 101
The Record Hall
16–16A Baldwin's Gardens
London EC1N 7RJ

www.spckpublishing.co.uk

Illustrations by Kathryn Wanless

EU GPSR Authorised Representative
LOGOS EUROPE, 9 rue Nicolas Poussin, 17000, La Rochelle, France
Email: Contact@logoseurope.eu

British Library Cataloguing-in-Publication Data
A catalogue record for this book is available from the British Library

ISBN 978-0-281-09151-5

10 9 8 7 6 5 4 3 2 1

Typeset by Fakenham Prepress Solutions
First printed in China by Dream Colour (Hong Kong) Printing Ltd

Produced on paper from sustainable sources

For Jesse and Isaac
I pray that you never stop drawing near to God

CONTENTS

INTRODUCTION

I didn't do GCSE art. It's not that I didn't enjoy the creativity of it all. It's that when my art teacher wasn't confiscating my non-regulation purple scarf, she was telling me how bad I was at it. I tried everything to get her to compliment my attempts, but I rarely broke the ceiling of a fifty per cent grade. That's a pass, but only just.

She did once give me eighty-five per cent. I would have been delighted if it hadn't been the one time I traced my sister's work from the year before. It's fair to say that she's the artist in the family. But maybe that's why I'm the one pulling this book together for you rather than her. Artist I am not, but that doesn't mean I don't feel a deep sense of peace when I give it a go.

For me, the Covid lockdowns of 2020–21 provided an opportunity to butcher my way through any and every craft and hobby going; I knitted, Sporcled, roller-skated, embroidered, flower-arranged, Duolingoed, baked, sketched, quizzed, pianoed, wrote and painted-by-numbers. Did I master any of them? Don't be silly. But I did enjoy them, and in many cases the gentle distraction and sense of calm they brought facilitated a moment of prayer;

sometimes a quick sentence, and at other times a longer conversation.

Prayer is hard. I admire the mystics who took themselves out into the forest with just a cape on their backs and the Holy Spirit in their hearts to sit in silence and solitude. Maybe one day, when I grow up, I'll manage twenty straight minutes of prayer without deciding I need a snack and taking a mental tour through my fridge. In the meantime, I enjoy combining my time with God with normal everyday tasks: brushing my teeth, taking a walk, preparing food and, more recently, drawing.

I sketch and create while casually chatting to God as if he's sitting next to me in art class. Only this time Miss Kennedy isn't there to shush me. I tell him about my day, pause to hear his encouragement or gentle correction. I thank him for what is good and vent if I'm not in a place to feel grateful. I reflect on my actions, repenting and apologising to God when I feel convicted, and this sometimes leads me to say sorry to someone else too. I chat to God about my friends, asking what they need, how I can help, who could do with a message or a gift or an extra prayer that day. And all this while running my pencil over the paper.

When I'm done, I step back and look at my work. It won't spark a bidding war between the Louvre and the Tate. It won't be hung in a royal palace, a suitable gift for a king. But I just know that if there are fridges in heaven, God already has a magnet in his hand as I offer it to him. He doesn't want the eighty-five per cent grade drawing that I copied. He wants the fifty per cent sketch that I did on my own. And that's all he wants from you too.

So, kettle on, comfy chair, 3B pencil in hand. This is an invitation to draw in to God while drawing.

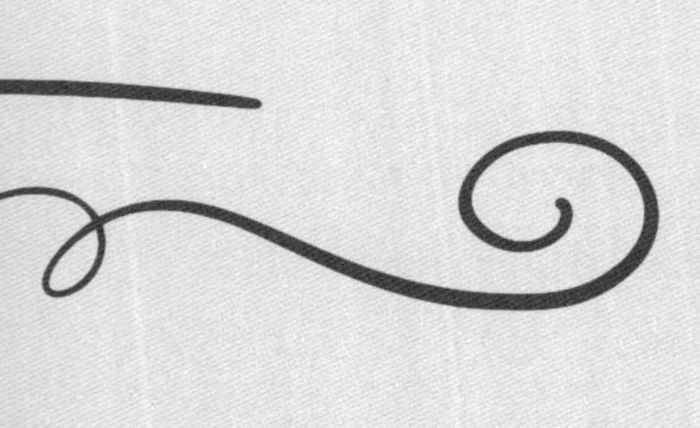

GRATITUDE

There's no better place to kick this off than with gratitude. No matter what our circumstances we are called to praise God. In this first section, we'll be thankful in prayer.

BREATHE

And let the peace that comes from Christ rule in your hearts. For as members of one body you are called to live in peace. And always be thankful.

(Colossians 3:15)

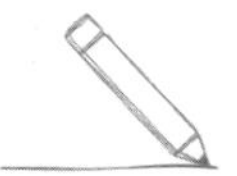

Let's start simple and just breathe. It's funny that as soon as someone tells me to breathe, I wonder if I ever knew how. This is an opportunity to welcome in a sense of stillness. Let your pencil mimic your breaths as you draw. Take a deep breath and let the squiggles and lines from your pencil reflect the slow and peaceful inhalation and exhalation.

GRATEFULNESS

And whatever you do or say, do it as a representative of the Lord Jesus, giving thanks through him to God the Father.
(Colossians 3:17)

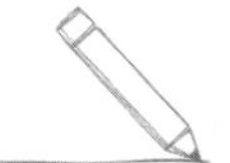

If I were embracing complete, unbridled honesty, I would be hard pushed to say I represent God well in all I do. It's why I don't put a Christian bumper sticker on my car – I don't think Jesus would want to be associated with my driving. But we *are* his representatives, and ideally we would be giving thanks to him in all we say and do (even driving).

Draw the back of a car and add in a bumper sticker that points to God in some way. While you draw, ask God how you can represent him better in your day-to-day life.

NAMES

I will praise you forever, O God, for what you have done. I will trust in your good name in the presence of your faithful people.
(Psalm 52:9)

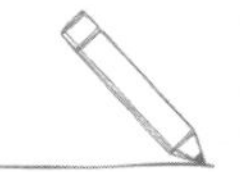

Names are big for God. He often changes the names of people in the Bible to signify a new start and chapter. There are lots of different names for God in the Bible: Abba, Alpha and Omega, Immanuel, Jehovah and many more. Pick your favourite and draw it out here. Take your time over the lettering and adorn it however you like. As you draw, speak to God about the power and majesty of his name and ask him to reveal more of his nature through it.

SAYING GRACE

So whether you eat or drink, or whatever you do, do it all for the glory of God.

(1 Corinthians 10:31)

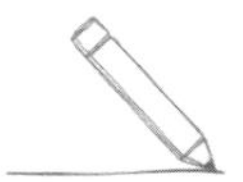

When it comes to saying thank you to God, many of us are most familiar with the practice before a meal. Saying grace may be a habit for those who grew up in a Christian household.

Draw your favourite plate of food, the drink you would have with it and the place setting. As you draw, speak to God about the many beautiful meals he's provided you with over the years and ask him how you can continue to bring him glory through hospitality.

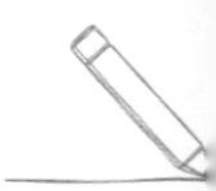

GOOD GIFTS

Whatever is good and perfect is a gift coming down to us from God our Father, who created all the lights in the heavens. He never changes or casts a shifting shadow.
(James 1:17)

The idea that all good gifts come from God is one that I often forget to engage with. Lots of us are quick to question God when we see the bad things around us, but how often do we praise him for the good?

Take the opportunity now to draw a big pile of presents. As you draw, ponder on how every good thing comes from him and thank him for the way he provides.

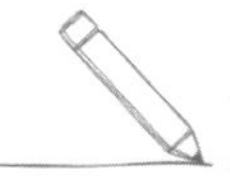

THE LIGHT

. . . always thanking the Father. He has enabled you to share in the inheritance that belongs to his people, who live in the light.
(Colossians 1:12)

Living in the light feels difficult when you're surrounded by darkness. But even if it involves some up-front honesty and repentance, it pays dividends in the long run.

Draw something that brings light: a candle, a campfire, a lamp or anything else you like. As you draw, thank God for the invitation to live in his light and ask him to show you anything in your life that could do with coming out of the dark.

GALLERY OF GOODNESS

O LORD, what a variety of things you have made! In wisdom you have made them all. The earth is full of your creatures.
(Psalm 104:24)

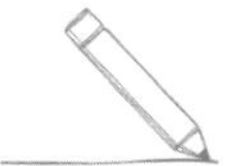

Our God is one of vast creativity. Let's celebrate that. Fill each of the frames in this gallery with a drawing of something God created. It could be a creature, a landscape, a plant or anything else. Thank God for his beautiful design as you draw.

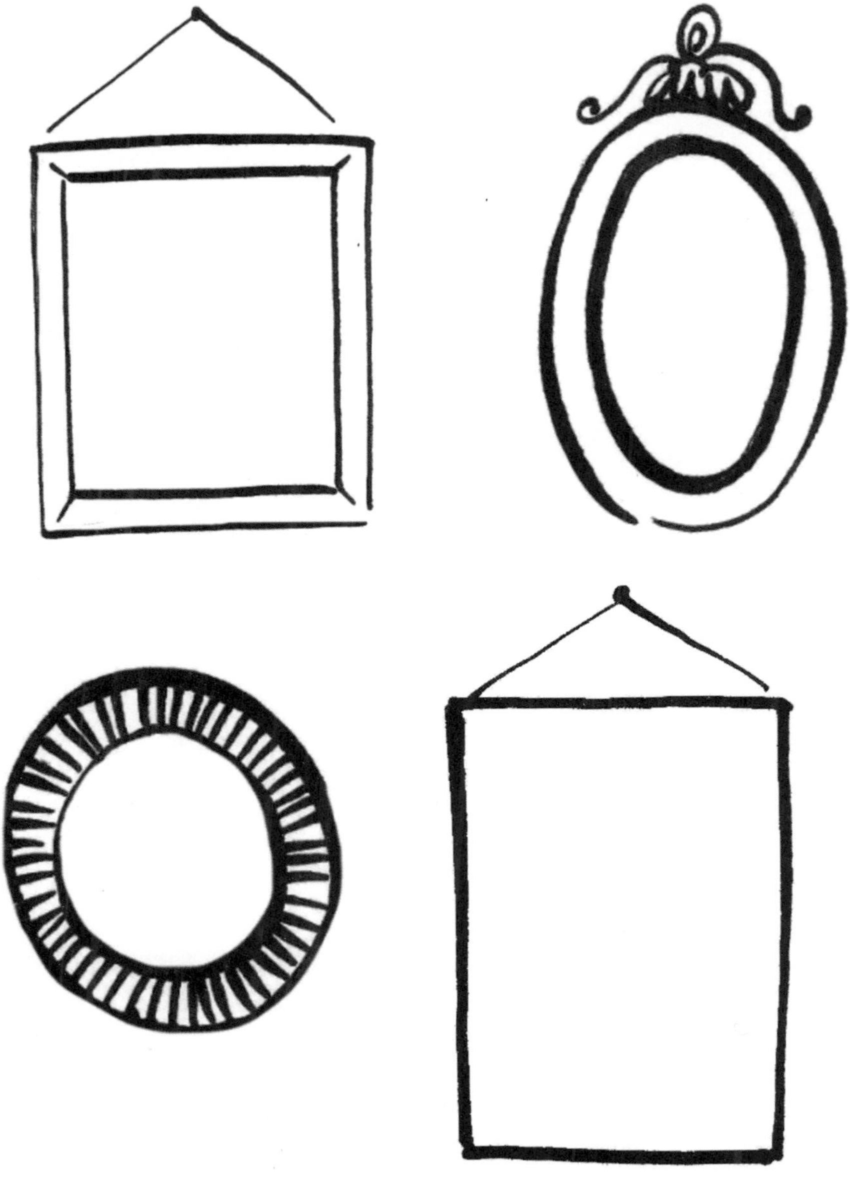

WELCOME

Enter his gates with thanksgiving; go into his courts with praise. Give thanks to him and praise his name.
(Psalm 100:4)

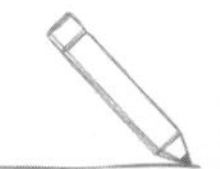

The welcome into God's courts (heaven) is the best invite we're ever going to get. There's no ticket ballot or queue on Ticketmaster; it's freely given and our company is deeply desired. Let's thank God for that – for the way he flings open the gates, even to those who struggle to feel wanted in everyday life.

Draw the grandest gates you can imagine. Make them stunning and ornate in whatever way you like, but make sure they're open. As you draw, thank God for the way he invites us into his courts.

THE GOOD SHEPHERD

Then we your people, the sheep of your pasture, will thank you forever and ever, praising your greatness from generation to generation.
(Psalm 79:13)

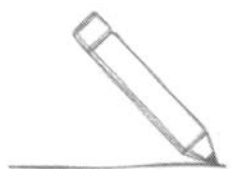

Jesus is described as the Good Shepherd, which makes us his flock. Just like sheep can't survive without their carer and protector, we need a shepherd.

Draw a sheep. As you do this, thank God for his provision and kindness to us in our helplessness.

LIPS

Therefore, let us offer through Jesus a continual sacrifice of praise to God, proclaiming our allegiance to his name.
(Hebrews 13:15)

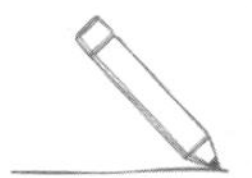

What we say matters. I am definitely prone to talking nonsense from time to time. But we're instructed in Hebrews to proclaim our allegiance to God. Talking about God is never just filling silence for the sake of it.

Draw a picture of lips – yours or someone else's. As you draw, ask God how you can better use your words to serve him.

SINGING

I will thank the LORD because he is just; I will sing praise to the name of the LORD Most High.
(Psalm 7:17)

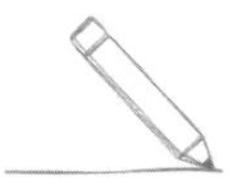

I love singing in church. I'm not talented enough to be in the band (although I'm pretty sure I could play the cajon – it's just a box, after all). But when all the instruments and voices join together, however amateurishly, something special happens.

Take time now to draw some instruments – ones you play or just ones you like. As you draw, praise God. You could sing if it's your thing, or pop a worship playlist on and let someone else do it for you.

BEAUTY FROM PAIN

We can rejoice, too, when we run into problems and trials, for we know that they help us develop endurance. And endurance develops strength of character, and character strengthens our confident hope of salvation. And this hope will not lead to disappointment. For we know how dearly God loves us, because he has given us the Holy Spirit to fill our hearts with his love.
(Romans 5:3–5)

God can turn any trial or trouble to his good. We're encouraged to rejoice in our difficulties, because our all-powerful God will use them to help us grow. I remember once hearing a preacher say, 'The world is broken; we're just called to plant flowers in the cracks.' So let's do that.

Much like the world, there are some cracks provided here. Draw some flowers growing from them. As you do this, ask God to turn a situation you're finding hard into something beautiful.

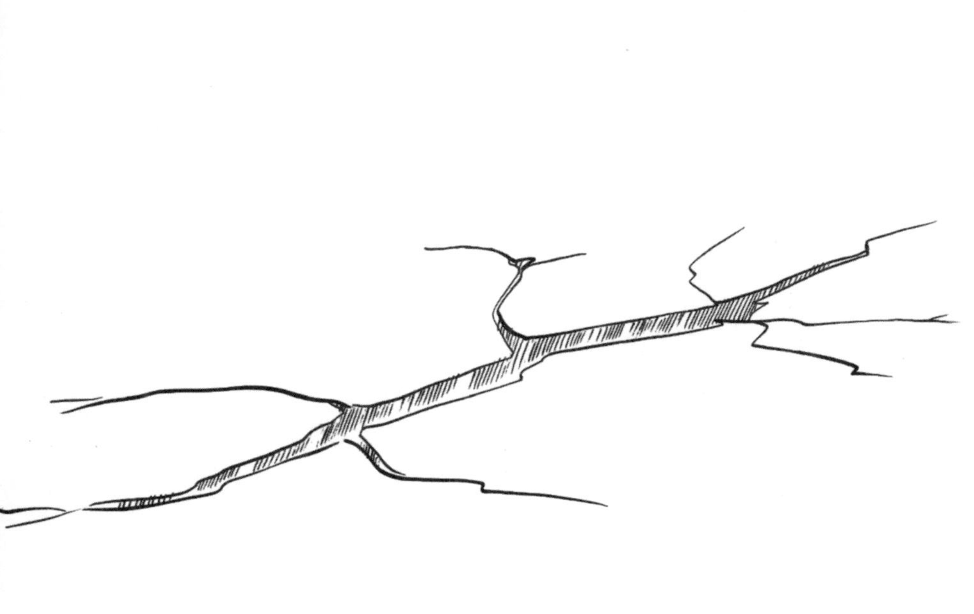

OUR SHIELD

The Lord is my strength and shield. I trust him with all my heart. He helps me, and my heart is filled with joy. I burst out in songs of thanksgiving.
(Psalm 28:7)

We all need a dose of God's strength. While people, whether with good or bad intentions, will let you down, God never will. He's a safe pair of hands in which to place your heart. And if any shield is going to keep you covered, it's God's.

Draw a shield. Make it big and strong and secure, just like the cover that God offers you. As you pray, thank him that you get access to his unending strength.

HAND IT OVER

Don't worry about anything; instead, pray about everything. Tell God what you need, and thank him for all he has done.
(Philippians 4:6)

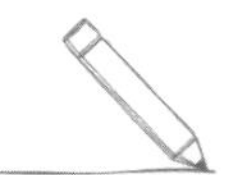

When it comes to worrying, just being told not to hasn't tended to help me in the past. But rather than seeing this verse as an instruction, I see it as a comforting invitation. It's God saying that he can carry our worries so we don't need to.

Draw your hands, palms open, and talk to God about the worries he is asking you to entrust to him in prayer.

GOD'S FEAST

You prepare a feast for me in the presence of my enemies. You honor me by anointing my head with oil. My cup overflows with blessings. (Psalm 23:5)

The Bible talks about God preparing a great feast for those who love him. On the facing page is an empty table. Draw on to it all the things that you imagine would be on a beautiful feasting table to share with God. As you draw, thank him for the gifts and blessings he's laid before you and those he's preparing. Be as imaginative as you like. It can be your favourite foods, delicious drinks, candles or even a dog sitting under the table to warm your feet.

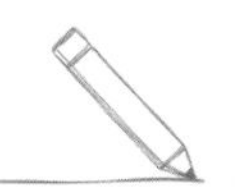

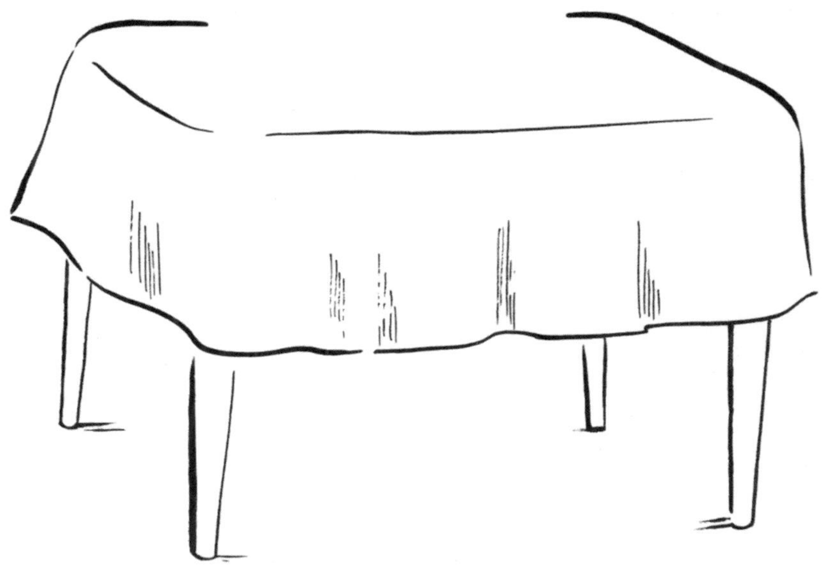

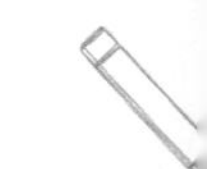

THE THRONE OF GOD

And they said, 'We give thanks to you, Lord God, the Almighty, the one who is and who always was, for now you have assumed your great power and have begun to reign.'
(Revelation 11:17)

There's so much comfort in knowing that God reigns supreme and will do for ever.

Draw a throne. As you draw, thank God for his omnipotence and that, despite his dominion, he wants to hear from you.

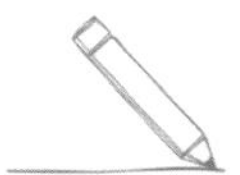

BEAUTY

He holds in his hands the depths of the earth and the mightiest mountains. The sea belongs to him, for he made it. His hands formed the dry land, too.
(Psalm 95:4–5)

We are surrounded by so much beauty and all of it points to God.

Draw your favourite type of landscape. That could be the sun-kissed sea, an awesome mountain range, lush green forests or anywhere else. As you draw, reflect on the beautiful things you've seen on trips, but also the beauty that is right on your doorstep.

UGLY?

Since everything God created is good, we should not reject any of it but receive it with thanks.
(1 Timothy 4:4)

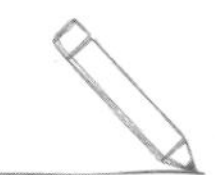

We often think about how God created everything good and beautiful, but there are a fair number of things in his creation that aren't what we would call conventionally attractive. Have you ever Googled a blobfish? Or a naked mole-rat? The fact is, we need to marvel at God's creation even when it doesn't look the way we'd like it to.

So draw some 'ugly' things and as you do this, ask God for his eyes to see the beauty in every single element of his creation.

ROOTED IN CHRIST

Let your roots grow down into him, and let your lives be built on him. Then your faith will grow strong in the truth you were taught, and you will overflow with thankfulness.
(Colossians 2:7)

Ultimately, we can itemise all the great things in the world and in our lives, but to feel true, deep and life-changing gratitude, we need to be in close contact with Jesus. The writer of Colossians, Paul, suggests that we allow our roots to grow down into him. Roots anchor a plant. They take in the food and water that keep the plant alive and help it survive when there are too few or too many of these nutrients around. We can get that same support and nourishment from God.

Add roots to the tree below. Make them vast and wide and strong, and at the end of each root, write something that God provides you with, for which you are grateful. Pray to him that you will continue to allow your roots to grow into him, benefiting from his support and care.

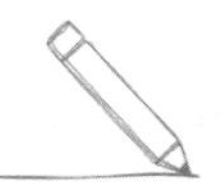

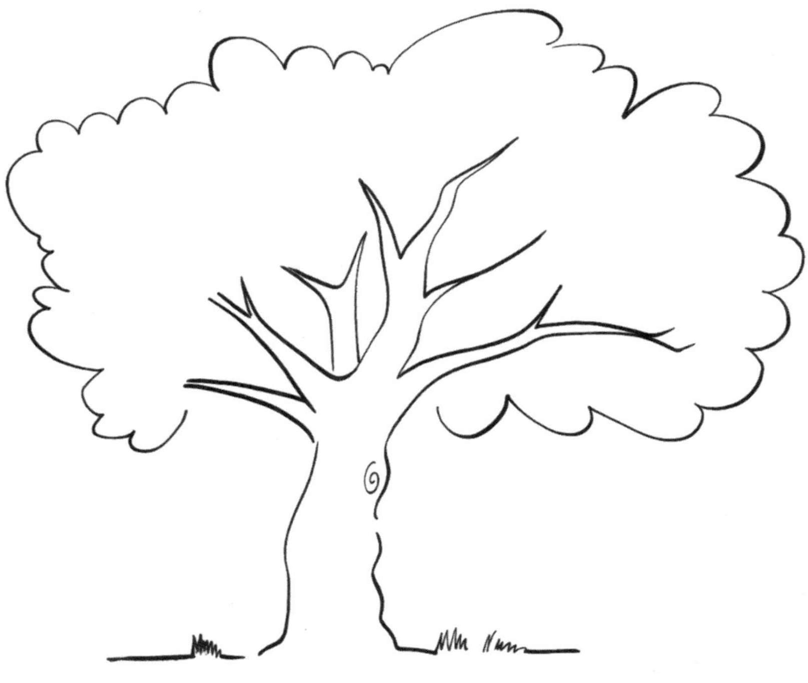

GOD

In this next section we're going to look at God's character and how we can grow in our understanding of who he is.

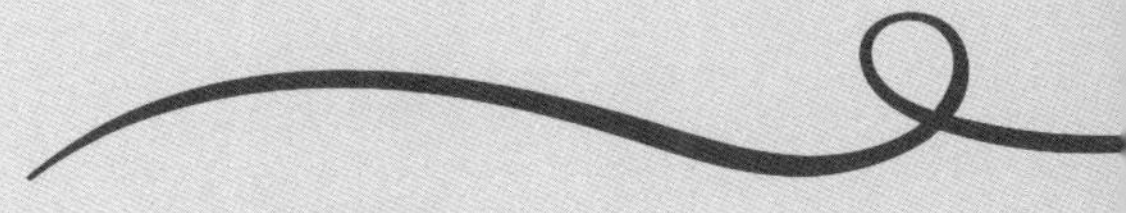

THE GOODNESS OF GOD

How great is the goodness you have stored up for those who fear you. You lavish it on those who come to you for protection, blessing them before the watching world.
(Psalm 31:19)

God doesn't just hand out a bit of goodness when we come to him. The Bible says he stores it up. He keeps a surplus ready for the people who love him – he's got more than enough to go around. He lavishes it on us. 'Lavish' isn't a word I use a lot, but what I'm hearing here is that he doesn't hold back.

Here are some storeroom shelves. At the moment they're empty, but you can fill them with all the jars and pots of goodness God has stockpiled just for you. As you do this, thank him for the way he wants to show us that goodness.

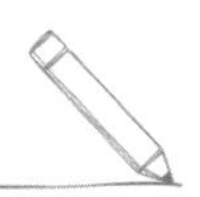

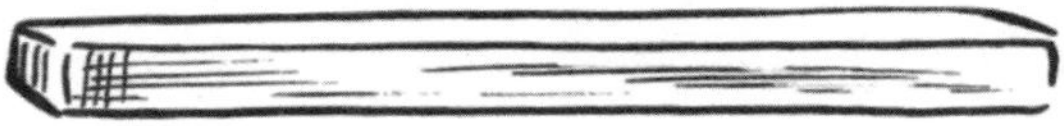

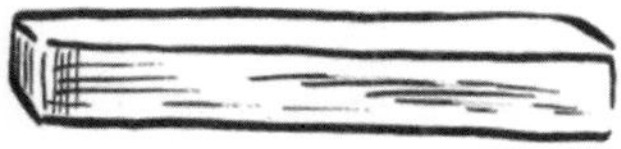

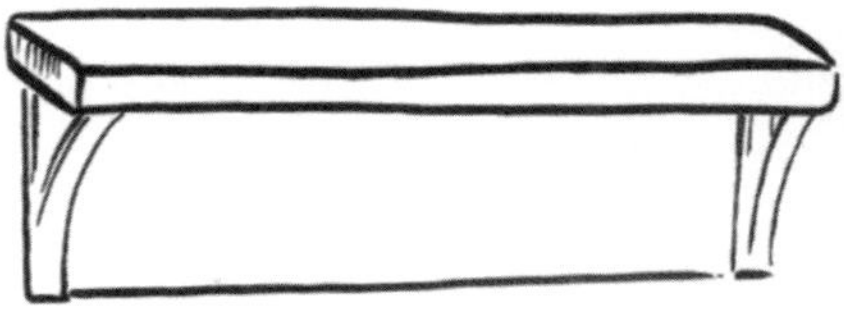

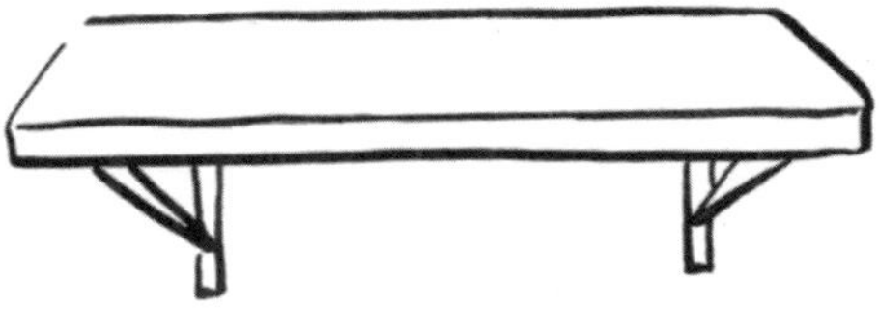

BRINGER OF HOPE

I pray that God, the source of hope, will fill you completely with joy and peace because you trust in him. Then you will overflow with confident hope through the power of the Holy Spirit.
(Romans 15:13)

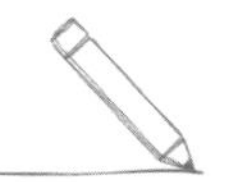

There's never a moment when we couldn't do with a bit more of God's hope. Even when things are going well, tapping into God, the source of hope, will always bring more peace and joy.

Draw something you've seen in this world that brings you hope for a better one. That could be a person who stood up for what they believed in, someone taking positive action, or a symbol like a rainbow or olive branch. Ask God to help you overflow with confident hope through the power of the Holy Spirit.

NURTURER

For the LORD your God is living among you. He is a mighty savior. He will take delight in you with gladness. With his love, he will calm all your fears. He will rejoice over you with joyful songs.
(Zephaniah 3:17)

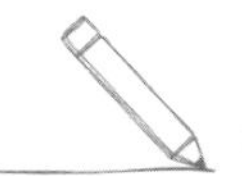

God wants to see us grow, and to do that he creates the right nurturing environment. He enjoys the good with us, soothes our fears and sings over us. We thrive when we feel celebrated and protected, and that's God's offer to us. It reminds me of houseplants – which in the spirit of honesty I should confess I often kill. But God doesn't.

Draw a selection of houseplants in lovely pots. As you draw, thank God that he provides everything we need in order to grow and thrive.

STRONG

But those who trust in the LORD will find new strength. They will soar high on wings like eagles. They will run and not grow weary. They will walk and not faint.
(Isaiah 40:31)

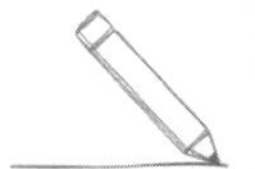

This has long been one of my go-to verses. When I feel low or discouraged, I picture myself on the eagle; a symbol of victory and power. That's *God's* victory and power, not mine. The fact that God is so strong and his strength doesn't deplete is a huge comfort to me given that mine is so infirm and short-lived!

Draw the eagle that God says he will empower us to replicate in our flying. Make it strong, fast and powerful. Thank God that his strength is such a gift to us.

MERCIFUL

The LORD is compassionate and merciful, slow to get angry and filled with unfailing love.
(Psalm 103:8)

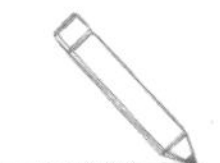

Being slow to anger is a growth area for me. Often when I'm frustrated with a friend, I can muster the compassion to remember their good and loving qualities. But if a big, faceless company keeps me on hold for forty-five minutes, you'd better believe my fury knows no bounds. Progress rather than perfection and all that.

Draw some things that make you disproportionately angry. It can be big or small, real or imagined. As you draw, pray that God would help you to embrace his mercy and patience, and that he would replace the anger with love. When you've finished drawing, mark it out with the symbol of the cross, signifying that you are leaving this anger with Jesus.

REDEEMER

He has removed our sins as far from us as the east is from the west.
(Psalm 103:12)

How we get to benefit from so much mercy and grace is beyond me. When we acknowledge our wrongdoing and commit to stopping the behaviour (that is, we repent), God moves it so far away from us that it doesn't need to be a part of our lives any more. He is the ultimate Redeemer.

On the east of the page, draw a box and label it 'sin', then draw yourself in the west – as far as the page allows! As you draw, thank God for his redemption.

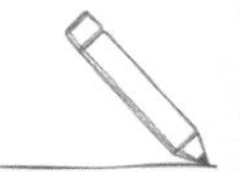

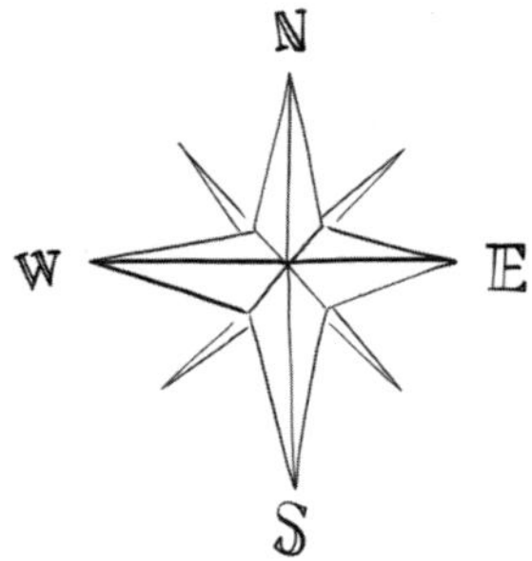
N
W
E
S

FATHER

See how very much our Father loves us, for he calls us his children, and that is what we are!
(1 John 3:1)

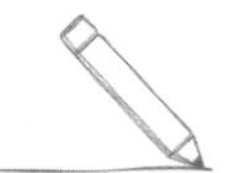

God is our Father, which means that, no matter what our age, we get to look to him. We get to experience things afresh and turn to him for reassurance. We're encouraged to continue to look at the world with this childlike wonder, knowing we have the safety of our Father to fall back on.

Draw some things you loved as a child to remind you of how exciting it was to discover new things. As you draw, thank God that he looks over us as we explore and venture out.

COMFORTER

When doubts filled my mind, your comfort gave me renewed hope and cheer.
(Psalm 94:19)

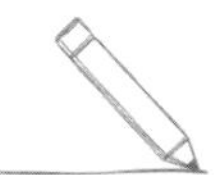

God sees when we're down and, if we let him, can bring us renewed hope and cheer. I remember someone who was in a moment of crisis saying, 'I know God is there, but I can't feel his arms around me.' I've found it hard to accept comfort from God when I can't physically feel him. But when we invite it in, his renewed hope and cheer can be more tangible than anything we would get from this world.

Draw some physical things that brings you comfort – your favourite food or drink, a friend, a hot bath or anything else. As you draw, thank God that his comfort is so much greater.

LIBERATOR

For the Lord is the Spirit, and wherever the Spirit of the Lord is, there is freedom.

(2 Corinthians 3:17)

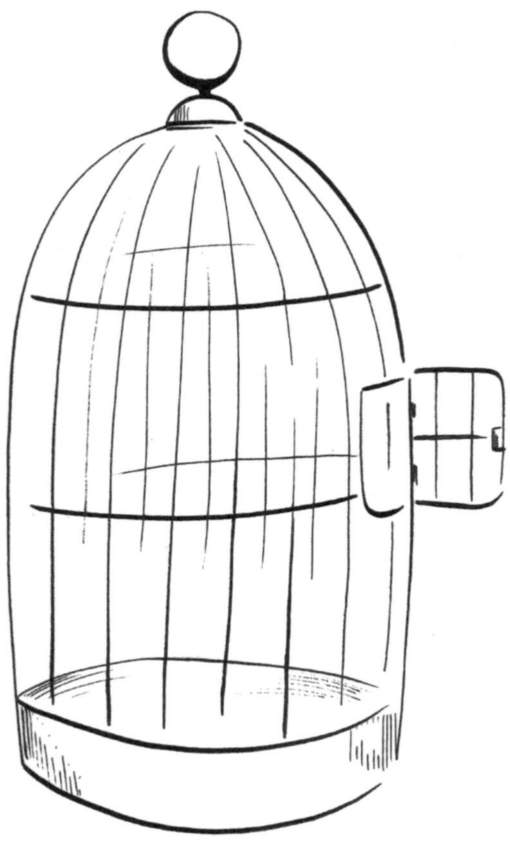

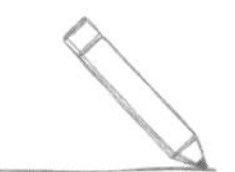

God brings freedom. For many of us, this won't look like physically breaking chains and kicking down the doors to locked rooms, but we are often slaves to our fears, poor behaviours and damaging thought processes. Jesus wants to liberate us from these things so that we can live life in all its fullness as he intended.

Opposite is a cage. You'll notice that the door is open. Draw something that has broken free of the cage – a bird, an animal, yourself even! As you do this, pray that God would bring to mind anything he wants you to find freedom from, and that he would help you take the next step towards that liberation.

CREATOR

For through him God created everything in the heavenly realms and on earth. He made the things we can see and the things we can't see – such as thrones, kingdoms, rulers, and authorities in the unseen world. Everything was created through him and for him.
(Colossians 1:16)

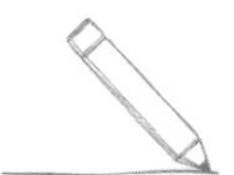

We've touched on our gratitude for God's creation already, but let's just take another moment to marvel at it. He literally created everything. There will never be a person whose creativity could match even one per cent of what we see from God.

Reflect on God as the ultimate Creator by drawing the most beautiful scene in nature that you've ever witnessed. It can be an imagined collection of all your favourite landscapes, or one specific beautiful place.

SURPRISING

For I am about to do something new. See, I have already begun!
(Isaiah 43:19)

When I was newly Christian, I was blown away by the number of incredible 'coincidences' I experienced in those early days. For example, praying for Christian friends only to find the new girl who moved into my flat sitting two rows in front of me at church. My friend calls them God-incidences and they feel really special – as if God designed them just for me, knowing what mattered to me most, big or small.

Draw a jack-in-the-box popping out. (If you're too young to have played with one, you'll have to Google it.) As you draw, thank God for the inspiring ways he surprises you.

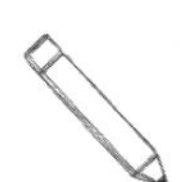

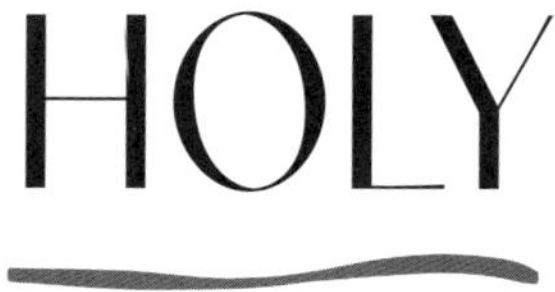

Who will not fear you, Lord, and glorify your name? For you alone are holy. All nations will come and worship before you, for your righteous deeds have been revealed.
(Revelation 15:4)

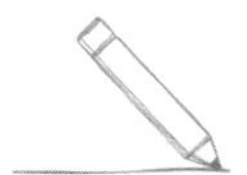

God is the definition of holy. Everything about him is sacred. I don't think we'll ever be able to understand the magnitude of that reality. But the fact that all nations will come and worship before him is a good start.

Let's draw the whole world, a globe packed full of people all called to worship our holy God. As you draw, praise him for his great holiness.

LOVE

But anyone who does not love does not know God, for God is love.
(1 John 4:8)

It's hard to grasp the nature of God, as we have such a narrow lens through which to view the world. But the aspect of his character I think we always allow to fall short from our perspective is love. I love Marmite and instant coffee (there's no place for judgement here), but that doesn't compare to how I love God or, more crucially, how God loves me.

The fact that we use the same word for both can cause us to underestimate the magnitude of God's love. This isn't a preference or a heart emoji. This is love that will kick down doors, start fires and refuse to rest, just to reach you. There is nothing that will stand in the way of it. You can't stop it. It is powerful and gentle all at the same time. There's nothing soppy or fanciful about it. This is love that can cause fighters to lay down their weapons and see criminals and addicts forever transformed.

Decorate this heart – the symbol of love – however you see fit. But don't confuse this with colouring in the front of a Valentine's card. This is a declaration of the significance of a love that is so influential we will never be able to understand it. As you draw, thank God for this great love and pray that he will continue to reveal his loving nature to you.

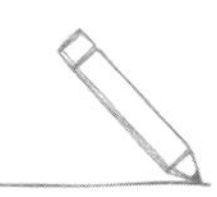

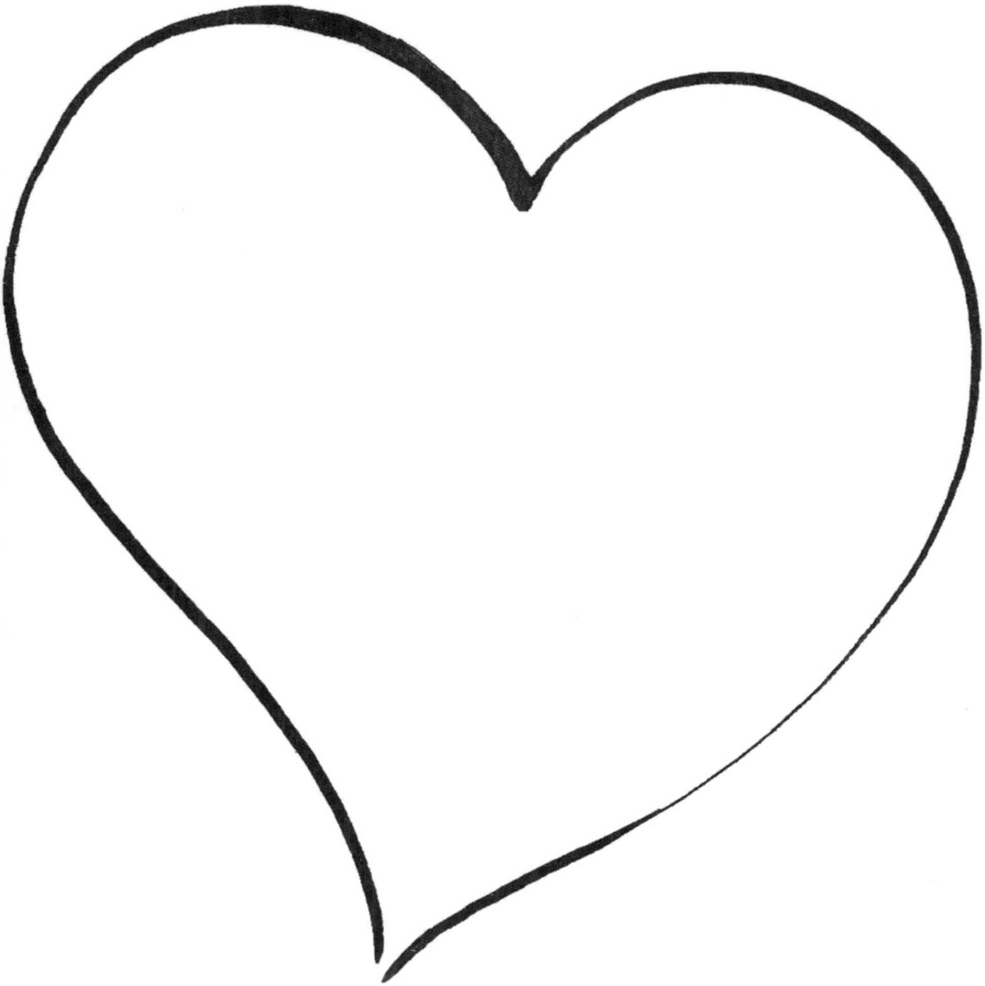

SEEKING AND FINDING GOD

'But from there you will search again for the LORD your God. And if you search for him with all your heart and soul, you will find him.'
(Deuteronomy 4:29)

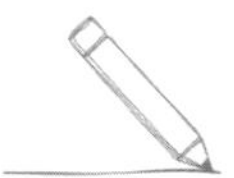

Finding and knowing God is an active choice. Just deciding we'd like to understand more about him isn't enough for us to grow in our understanding of God. Reading the Bible is obviously the usual place to start when we want to deepen our understanding of God, but prayer, church, other Christian books and Bible commentaries can all open up our understanding of him too.

Draw something that would help you on a mission of discovery – you know, the sort of thing you'd find in Dora the Explorer's backpack: binoculars, a torch, a rope, a magnifying glass, even a phone. As you draw, ask God to guide you as you continue to familiarise yourself with him.

FATHER AND SON

'If you had really known me, you would know who my Father is. From now on, you do know him and have seen him!'
(John 14:7)

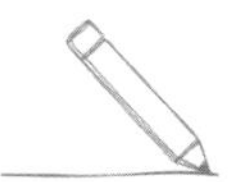

Lots of us struggle to reconcile the God we see in the Old Testament (doing all the smiting) with Jesus, whom we see as far gentler, in the New Testament. But the Bible is clear that they are one and the same, and every characteristic we see in Jesus is present in God.

Draw a father and son, with all their similarities, and as you do, pray that through your understanding of Jesus your understanding of God would grow.

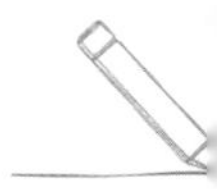

JESUS

'For no one can come to me unless the Father who sent me draws them to me, and at the last day I will raise them up.'
(John 6:44)

This is Jesus speaking as recorded in the Gospel of John.

Allow God to draw you to Jesus by drawing something you associate with him. For many that will be a cross, but what about something else he interacted with in his life? A donkey? A well? A bottle of perfume? Some water that didn't stay water for long?

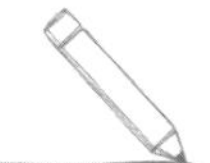

OPEN THE DOOR

'Look! I stand at the door and knock. If you hear my voice and open the door, I will come in, and we will share a meal together as friends.' (Revelation 3:20)

For years, Jesus was accessible in my life, knocking at the door, and I chose to ignore him. He wants a relationship with us. He wants to sit with us, to share a meal and to know us personally.

Draw a door handle. As you draw, pray that you would be able to hear Jesus' voice and that you would have the courage to boldly open the door and invite him in.

CALL INCOMING...

Don't worry about anything; instead, pray about everything. Tell God what you need, and thank him for all he has done.
(Philippians 4:6)

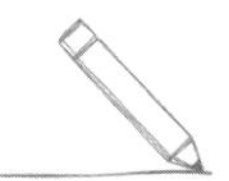

Imagine not worrying about anything and just handing everything over to God! That's the genuine invitation, albeit one that feels like a distant dream when the stresses come piling in. God sees us struggle and is so desperate for us to talk to him.

Draw a phone with God calling. As you draw, think about what you'd say to him on a call. Tell him what you need and thank him for what he's done.

HEARING FROM GOD

'Come to me with your ears wide open. Listen, and you will find life.'
(Isaiah 55:3)

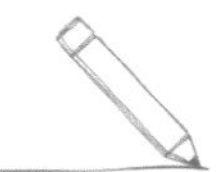

It's one thing to talk to God, but hearing from him always feels like a level up to me. It's taken me years to become more familiar with God's voice. God sometimes speaks to me through pictures, but often it's a nudge. It's what many people would call a 'gut feeling'. It's a deep sense of unease when I know I'm doing something wrong or I need to take action, followed by a deep sense of peace when I readjust according to his will.

Draw a radio. It can be a modern DAB or one of those old wind-up ones – whatever comes to mind. As you draw, pray to God that you would hear him better, and make sure to pause and give yourself space to listen.

YOU AND GOD

'If a man has a hundred sheep and one of them wanders away, what will he do? Won't he leave the ninety-nine others on the hills and go out to search for the one that is lost? And if he finds it, I tell you the truth, he will rejoice over it more than over the ninety-nine that didn't wander away! In the same way, it is not my heavenly Father's will that even one of these little ones should perish.'
(Matthew 18:12–14)

Many of us can't imagine God coming to seek us out directly, even leaving others in order to focus exclusively on us. But in this passage Jesus makes it clear that God will do what he can to bring us back if we wander away.

Draw an imagined map, adding in the streets and parks and any other landmarks you like. As you draw, thank God that he will always make a way for you to come home and that he will come and seek you out if necessary.

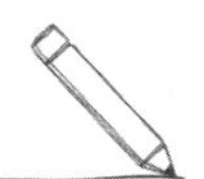

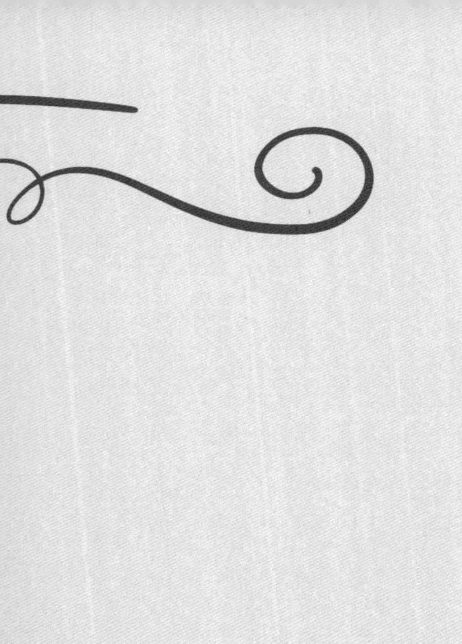

IDENTITY

Now that we've spent some time praying about who God is, let's spend some time speaking to God about who he says *we* are.

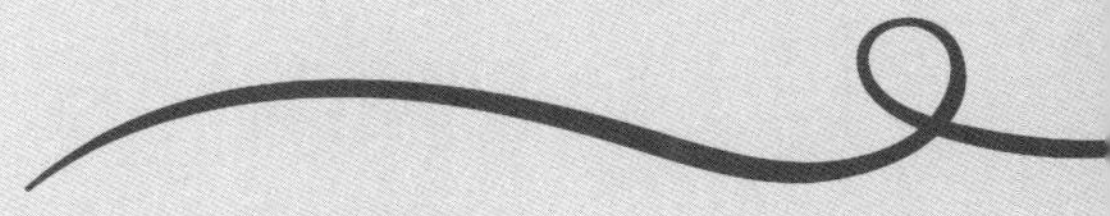

ROYALTY

But to all who believed him and accepted him, he gave the right to become children of God.
(John 1:12)

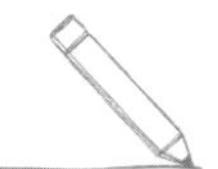

It's all very well being told that we are children of God, but how often do we act like it? How often do we conduct ourselves as though we're royalty and the children of the King?

Draw a picture of a crown – the ultimate royal accessory. As you draw, pray that you wouldn't just know in theory that you are a son or daughter of the King, but that you would actually believe it, deep down. And that you would act accordingly.

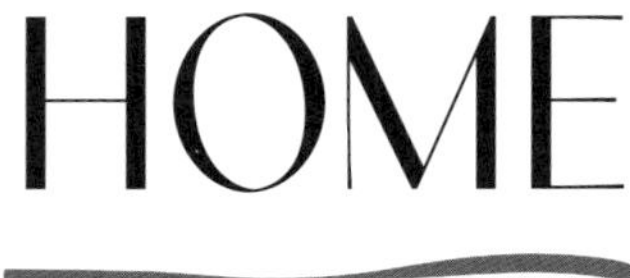

HOME

God decided in advance to adopt us into his own family by bringing us to himself through Jesus Christ. This is what he wanted to do, and it gave him great pleasure.
(Ephesians 1:5)

When it comes to God's house, plenty of us recognise that we're invited in, but we see ourselves as second-class citizens in his home. We look around and assume that other people have genuinely earned their place and we're lucky to have slipped in through the back door. But God hasn't asked you to join him just so you can clear the table once the others are done and then eat the leftovers. He takes pleasure in inviting you in as a guest of honour.

Draw your seat. It's the chair you will pull up as you take your place at God's table – just where he wants you.

COMPLETE

So you also are complete through your union with Christ, who is the head over every ruler and authority.
(Colossians 2:10)

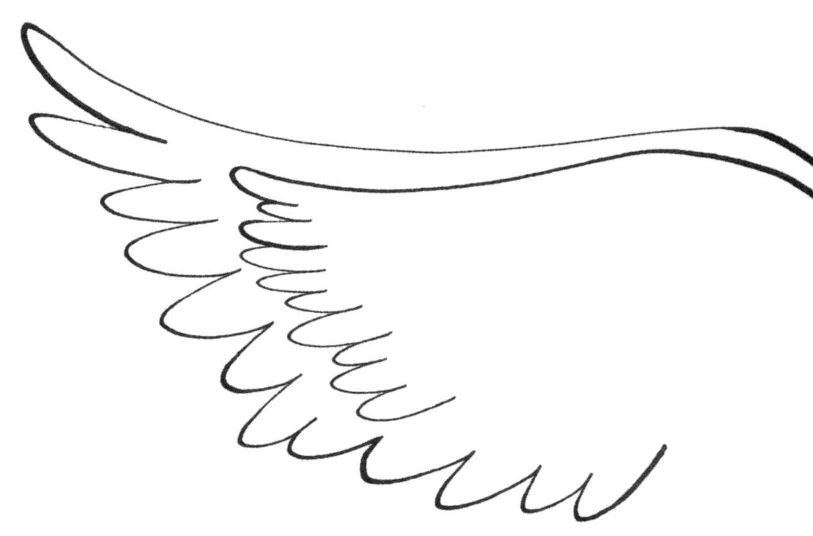

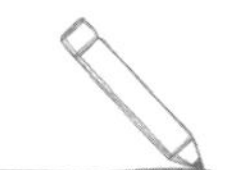

We spend our lives looking for that thing to complete us: a job, a home, an amount of money, a child or a partner (cue that awful line from Tom Cruise in *Jerry Maguire*). But God says we're complete through relationship with him.

Here is an incomplete drawing showing just one wing. Finish it however you like. As you draw, thank God that through him you are whole – with or without the things the world says you need.

SELF-PORTRAIT

So God created human beings in his own image. In the image of God he created them; male and female he created them.
(Genesis 1:27)

We can be our own worst critics, always seeing the bad in ourselves. Yes, we all have areas of our spiritual lives and characters that can do with work, but often we're so set on seeing where we're falling short that we don't see all the incredible gifts God has given us.

God doesn't make mistakes and he certainly didn't make a mistake when he created us. He knows every inch of our skin; every blemish, birthmark and freckle.

Take a moment to look in the mirror at God's creation – you. Admire yourself. Marvel at his creativity, and wonder at the way he made something so intricate and beautiful from nothing at all. You are God's masterpiece and it's time to use his artwork to create your own.

On the facing page, draw a self-portrait. Really take the time to look at the contours of your face and appreciate how God made you. As you draw, thank him for each feature and for the things it can do. Reflect on how your ears, eyes, nose and mouth allow you to interact with the world around you, and the experiences they have brought you. If there's something about your appearance that you don't like, or feel self-conscious about, pray about it as you draw. Ask for God to clear away the lies and to show you how he sees you. Ask him why he created you the way he did and allow space to hear from him.

DIFFERENT

But you are not like that, for you are a chosen people. You are royal priests, a holy nation, God's very own possession. As a result, you can show others the goodness of God, for he called you out of the darkness into his wonderful light.
(1 Peter 2:9)

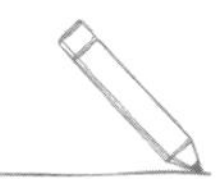

There's a lot of pressure from people around us to fit in. God makes it clear, though, that he's not looking for us to conform, but to stand out as chosen people. It's difficult to stand apart.

Draw something you enjoy that other people just don't get. For example, I will be drawing a picture of me watching Agatha Christie's *Miss Marple* while doing Killer Sudoku puzzles. Sure, it's not a conventionally fun activity, but I enjoy it. As you draw your version, pray that God would give you the confidence to show others his goodness by living differently.

LABELS

There is no longer Jew or Gentile, slave or free, male and female. For you are all one in Christ Jesus.
(Galatians 3:28)

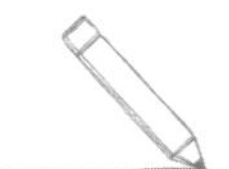

One of my favourite things about Jesus (of which there are many) is that he rejects the labels the world puts on us and levels the playing field. We can adopt so many unhelpful tags, many of which we need to cast off. For example, have you ever believed you are 'hard work', 'hard to love', 'unwanted' or 'unpopular'? Perhaps there are others that come to mind?

Draw some labels and tags. As you do this, pray that God would help you to cast these off and embrace your true identity through him instead.

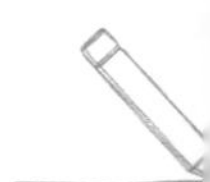

NEW LIFE

This means that anyone who belongs to Christ has become a new person. The old life is gone; a new life has begun!
(2 Corinthians 5:17)

You are never stuck. Never trapped. You've never gone so far down the wrong route that you can't turn back to God and embrace new life. And I say that as a recovering drug addict.

Draw a snake shedding its skin and stepping (or slithering) into new life. As you do this, pray that God would help you identify and shed the things that aren't serving you and him, and help you to be renewed.

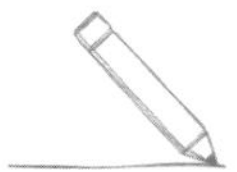

PEACE

The LORD gives his people strength. The LORD blesses them with peace. (Psalm 29:11)

We've already pondered God's strength, but our access to it should be a great source of peace.

As you reflect on God's blessing of peace, draw its biblical symbol – a dove. As you draw, thank God that you get to rest in his peace and welcome more of it into your life. We really can never get enough.

TREASURED

'For you are a holy people, who belong to the LORD your God. Of all the people on earth, the LORD your God has chosen you to be his own special treasure.'
(Deuteronomy 7:6)

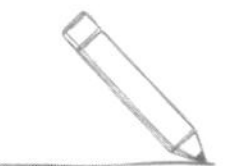

Can you imagine stumbling across a chest full of treasure? (From what I've read, this would likely be at the bottom of the sea.) The value of that chest and your excitement at having found it would be immeasurable. That's how God feels about us.

Fill this empty chest with treasure. Have it overflowing with gold, jewels and gems that spill out on to the facing page. As you draw, pray to God that you would see yourself how he sees you, with that immeasurable value.

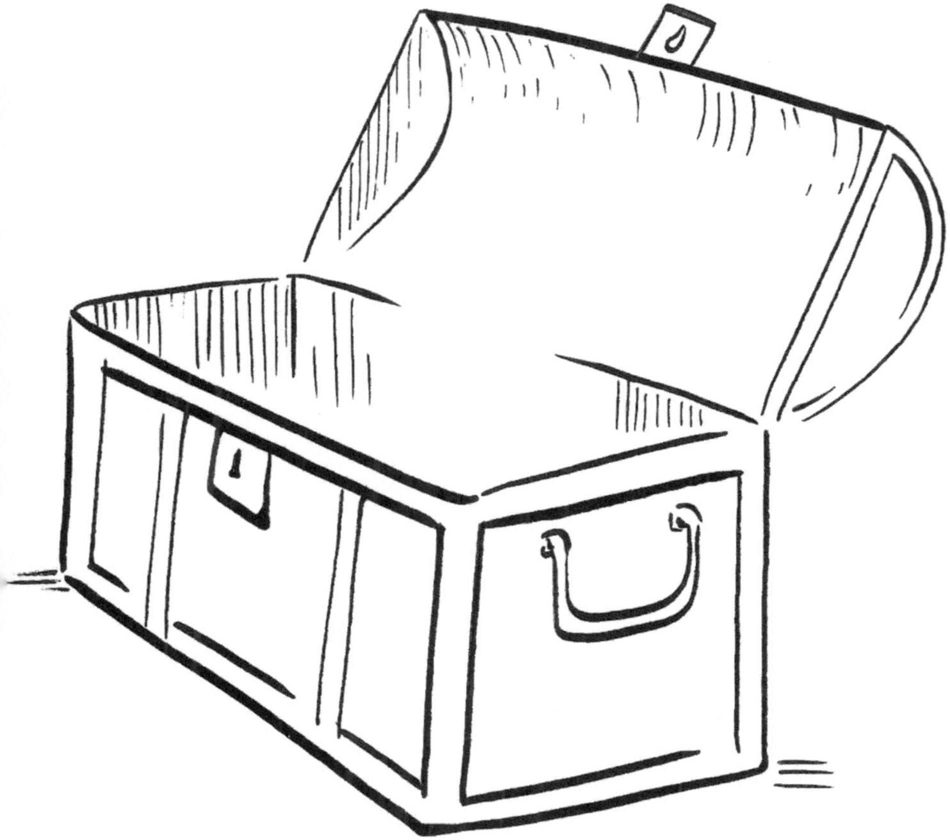

DELIGHT

For the LORD delights in his people; he crowns the humble with victory. (Psalm 149:4)

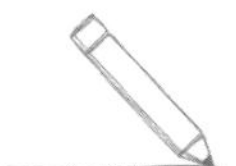

When it comes to delighting in things, I delight in puppies, babies I'm related to and a really well-made oat-milk latte. In that order. There have been times when I've found it hard to believe that I would be delightful to God. But the Bible is clear that we are.

Draw some things that delight you. As you draw, thank God that he is so delighted with you.

SPIRIT

For God has not given us a spirit of fear and timidity, but of power, love, and self-discipline.
(2 Timothy 1:7)

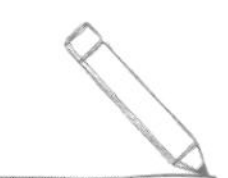

With God's strength and wisdom there is nothing we can't overcome. There is nothing to fear, even the biggest, most momentous challenges.

Take a moment now to draw a mountain. The biggest, most treacherous mountain you can imagine. As you draw, thank God that you don't need to be afraid of things that feel insurmountable when he is with you.

TOOLS

By his divine power, God has given us everything we need for living a godly life. We have received all of this by coming to know him, the one who called us to himself by means of his marvelous glory and excellence.
(2 Peter 1:3)

Through knowing God better, we are given everything we need to live a full life.

Below is an empty tool belt. Draw in a full set of tools. As you do, thank God for the way he has equipped you and pray that he continues to provide all you need.

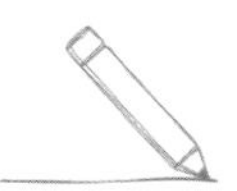

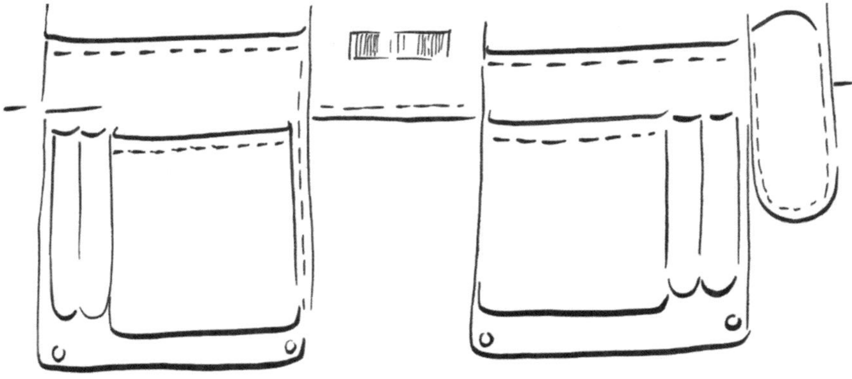

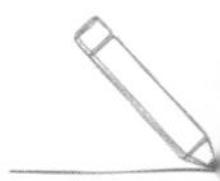

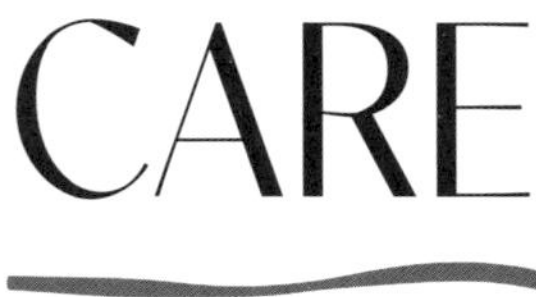

CARE

Don't you realize that your body is the temple of the Holy Spirit, who lives in you and was given to you by God?
(1 Corinthians 6:19)

Every time we do something to care for ourselves, we are looking after something God gave us.

Draw something that's a part of your self-care routine, whether that's a nice soap, some moisturiser, or even (and the Lord be with you) an ice-bath. As you draw, thank God for your body and the ways you and he look after it.

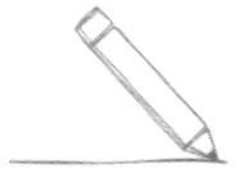

TALENTS

Do you have the gift of speaking? Then speak as though God himself were speaking through you. Do you have the gift of helping others? Do it with all the strength and energy that God supplies. Then everything you do will bring glory to God through Jesus Christ.
(1 Peter 4:11)

Each of us has a unique combination of talents and a unique set of opportunities to use them for Christ. What are your talents?

Draw yourself doing something you're good at. As you draw, ask God how you can use this talent to bring glory to him.

HAIR

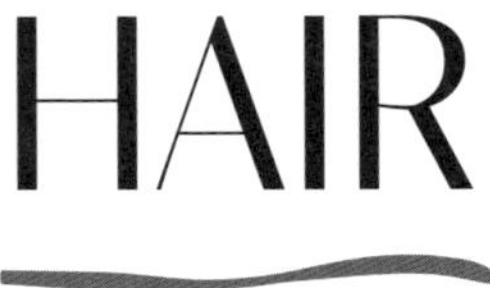

'And the very hairs on your head are all numbered. So don't be afraid; you are more valuable to God than a whole flock of sparrows.'
(Luke 12:7)

Knowing that God has numbered every one of my hairs is enough to have me reaching for the Tangle Teezer. But he's a God of the details, even down to a follicular level.

Opposite is a hairless head. Add hair to it in any style you like. As you draw, take care with each stroke. Every single one matters to God. Pray and thank him for his attention to detail.

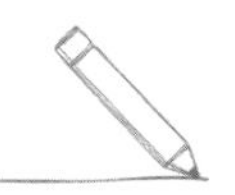

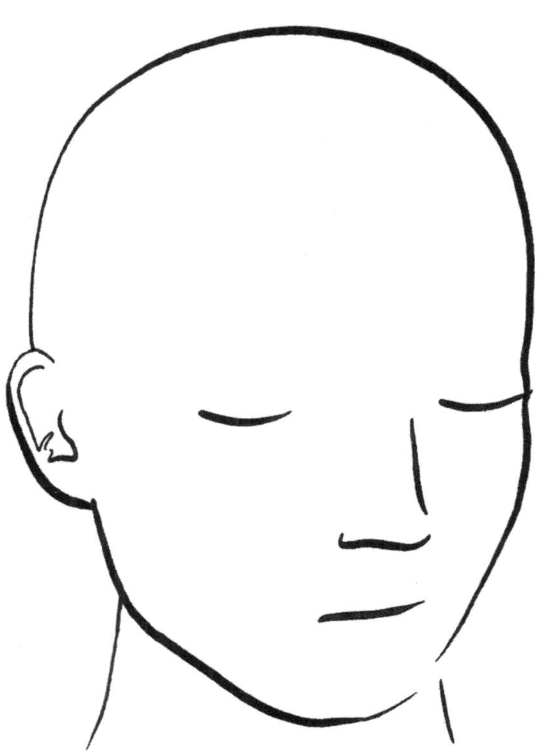

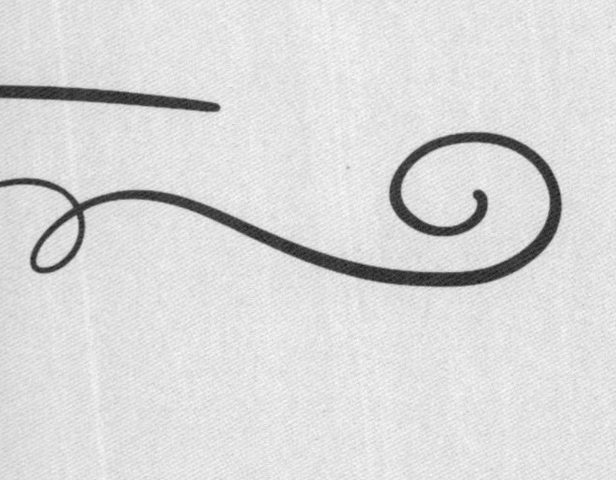

PURPOSE

With a better understanding of our identity in Christ, we're primed and ready to pray about our purpose and how we can best serve him.

BEARING FRUIT

'I am the true vine, and my Father is the gardener. He cuts off every branch in me that bears no fruit, while every branch that does bear fruit he prunes so that it will be even more fruitful.'
(John 15:1–2, NIV)

When God is prompting us to make changes or address something not right in our character, that pruning process can be painful. But after the cutting back comes the fruit.

Opposite is a tree that has been pruned right back. Take some time now to pray about the fruit that God wants to grow in you. Fill the branches with delicious ripe fruit in anticipation of how God will bring beautiful things into your life if you push through the difficult pruning.

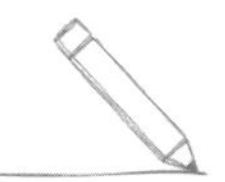

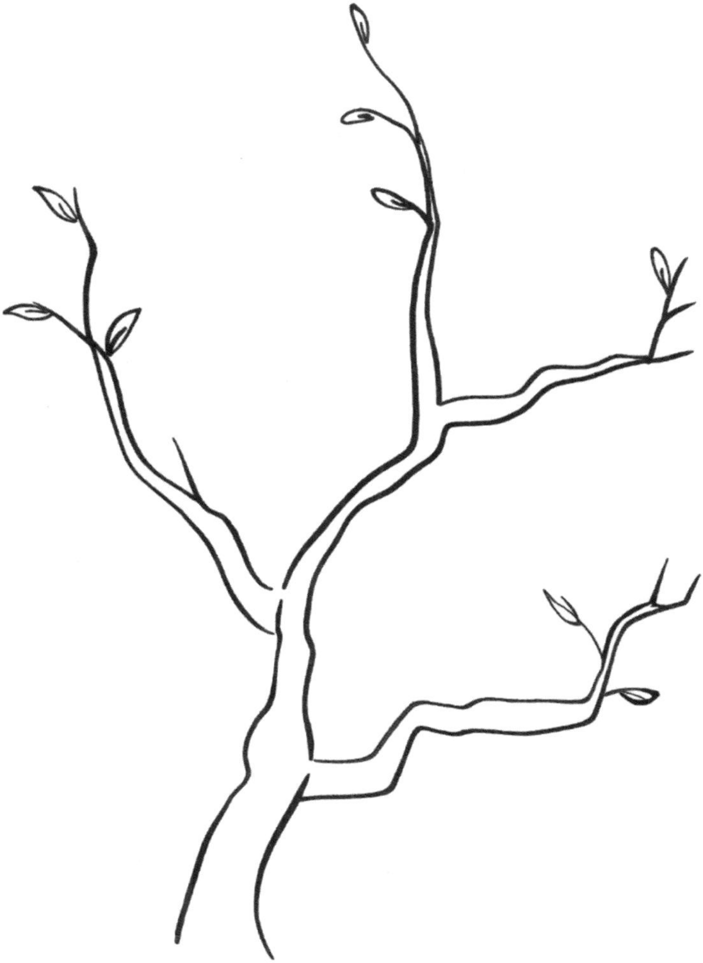

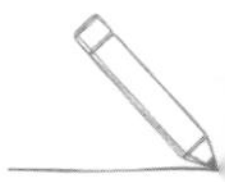

HEAVENLY EYES

So we don't look at the troubles we can see now; rather, we fix our gaze on things that cannot be seen. For the things we see now will soon be gone, but the things we cannot see will last forever.
(2 Corinthians 4:18)

We're encouraged to see things through heavenly eyes rather than from our limited perspective. But that's not always easy.

Draw a pair of eyes. As you draw, ask God to widen your perspective up to heaven. Pray for the vision to see things as he does.

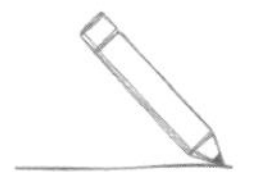

MASTERPIECE

For we are God's masterpiece. He has created us anew in Christ Jesus, so we can do the good things he planned for us long ago.
(Ephesians 2:10)

We were made by God and we are masterpieces. Even if we don't always feel like it.

Pick any famous painting and draw your own interpretation of it below. As you draw, thank God that he created you so well and for a purpose.

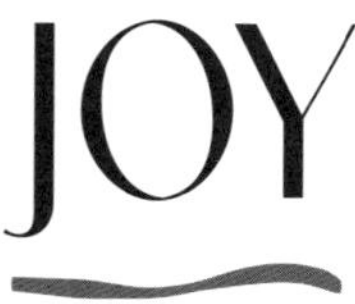

'I have told you these things so that you will be filled with my joy. Yes, your joy will overflow!'
(John 15:11)

Our enjoyment is important to God. Jesus wants us to be filled with joy – so much so that it overflows!

Below is an empty bucket. Fill it up with things that bring you joy. That could be your hobbies, favourite foods, your Bible or things that you treat yourself to. Just make sure the bucket overflows.

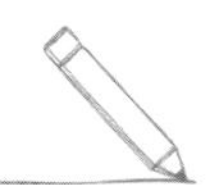

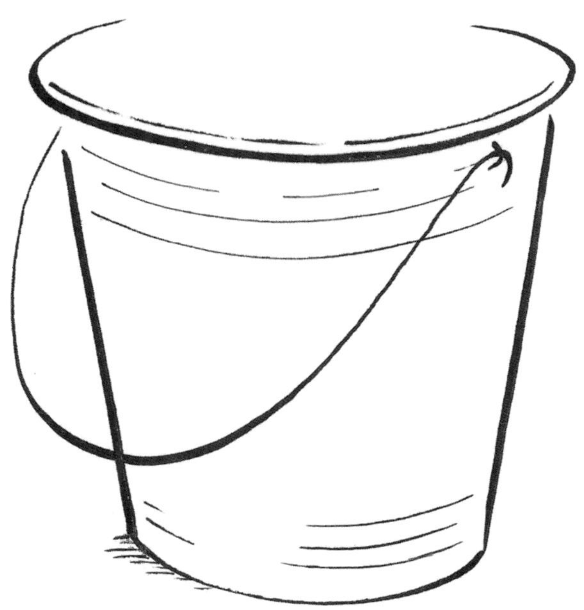

PLAYTIME

Then he said, 'I tell you the truth, unless you turn from your sins and become like little children, you will never get into the Kingdom of Heaven. So anyone who becomes as humble as this little child is the greatest in the Kingdom of Heaven.'
(Matthew 18:3–4)

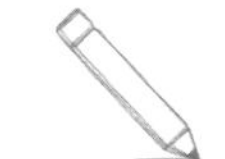

With the to-do lists, admin and hustle and bustle of life, it's easy to lose the sense of wonder we had as children. We quickly stop imagining and start worrying.

When you were younger, what job did you dream of doing? Draw yourself doing the work you imagined yourself doing as a child. As you draw, pray for your younger self, that you would be able to connect with the excitement and sense of discovery that you had then. If you feel that you've lost it, it's OK to grieve that loss and hand it over to God.

DO GOOD

Don’t let evil conquer you, but conquer evil by doing good.
(Romans 12:21)

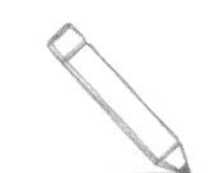

Our actions are important. God's not looking for followers who just pay him lip service but then don't consider him in the way they behave.

Draw a picture of something good you could do. Perhaps that's a favour you could do for someone, a meal you could make them or a gift that would help them out. As you draw, pray that God would show you some small ways you can do good today.

PLAYING THE FOOL

So be careful how you live. Don't live like fools, but like those who are wise. Make the most of every opportunity in these evil days.
(Ephesians 5:15–16)

I heard a woman telling off her son on Instagram, saying, 'Wisdom is chasing you, but you run faster.' Sometimes I worry I run too fast too! We can all fail to act wisely from time to time. But we are called to carefully consider our opportunities and, with God's guidance, make the most of them for him.

Draw a picture of a clown or court jester. As you draw, pray that God would steer you away from any foolishness and show you his wisdom.

HANDING OVER

You can make many plans, but the LORD's purpose will prevail. (Proverbs 19:21)

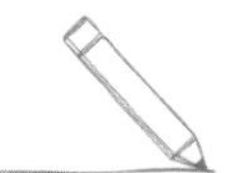

You might have heard the saying 'If you want to make God laugh, tell him your plans'. This feels a little harsh. I doubt God's sitting up there looking at my to-do list and chuckling to himself. But it does illustrate how often our plans aren't his and how often we will have to let ours go.

Draw a gold medal. As you draw, reflect on how God's plans need to take first place. Pray that he would help you to submit to his plan and allow your plans to take silver.

SEASONS

For everything there is a season, a time for every activity under heaven.
(Ecclesiastes 3:1)

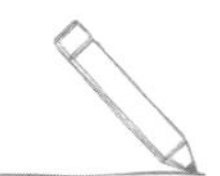

The fact that there is a time for everything – both good and bad – is an encouragement to me.

Draw a scene from your favourite annual season below. As you do, talk to God about the spiritual season you're in and what joys and challenges it brings. If it's a tough one, pray that you would move through it with him, and if it's a good one, pray that you would be able to fully enjoy it.

ACT NOW

'Who knows if perhaps you were made queen for just such a time as this?'
(Esther 4:14)

Sometimes the time is now. Sometimes you've done all the preparation God intended and it's time to take action. Sometimes you have been deliberately placed where you are for such a time as this.

Draw a grandfather clock. As you draw, ask God if this is one of those times for you. Speak to God about what action you might take and why the time is now.

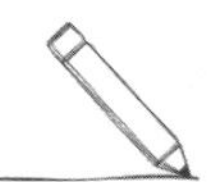

TRUST

'For I know the plans I have for you,' says the LORD. 'They are plans for good and not for disaster, to give you a future and a hope.'
(Jeremiah 29:11)

Trusting that God knows what's ahead means that sometimes we have to take some blind corners, not knowing what's around that bend. But God knows and he's got a plan.

Draw a road with a blind corner ahead. As you draw, ask God that he would keep you safe as you walk the path he's laid out for you, and that you would trust in his plan.

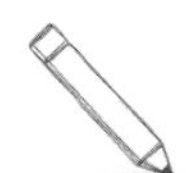

SEND ME

Then I heard the Lord asking, 'Whom should I send as a messenger to this people? Who will go for us?' I said, 'Here I am. Send me.'
(Isaiah 6:8)

We know that God wants to use us for his mission and purpose, but it can be hard to step up and willingly give ourselves over – especially if it means walking into the unknown.

Draw whatever you like on the front of this blank postcard. On the back write a simple prayer to God telling him to send you. As you draw, pray that God would increase your trust in him so that you can truly say 'send me' and mean it.

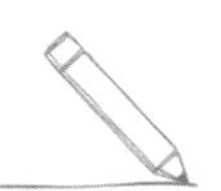

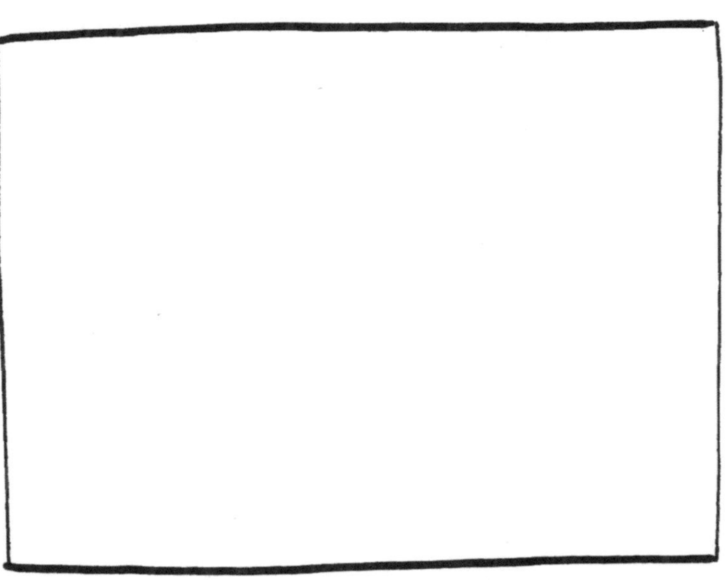

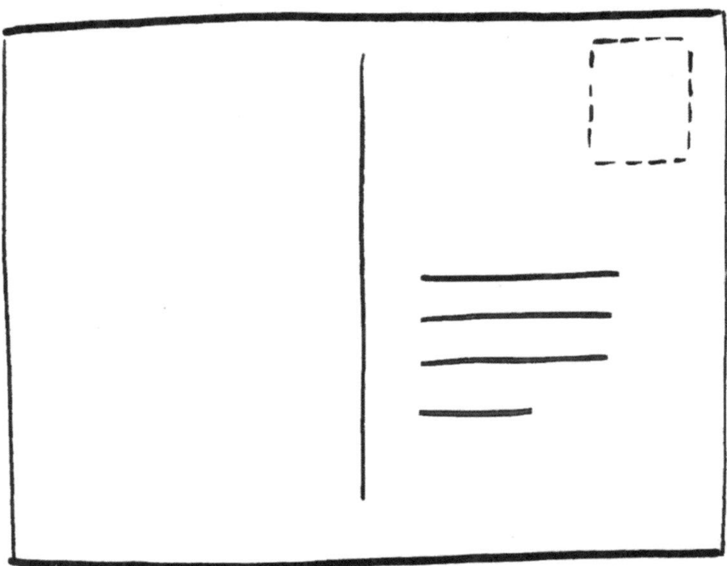

COMMISSION

Jesus came and told his disciples, 'I have been given all authority in heaven and on earth. Therefore, go and make disciples of all the nations, baptizing them in the name of the Father and the Son and the Holy Spirit. Teach these new disciples to obey all the commands I have given you. And be sure of this: I am with you always, even to the end of the age.'
(Matthew 28:18–20)

Known as the Great Commission, this was the moment Jesus told people to go and share the gospel and baptise others. Being baptised in water is a symbol of Jesus Christ's death, burial and resurrection.

Draw a place where people can be baptised. That could be a swimming pool, the sea, a lake or – if your church is anything like mine – an inflatable paddling pool! As you do, pray about the significance of baptism. Ask God if it's time for you to be baptised or to reaffirm the promises you made when you were.

OBEDIENCE

But those who obey God's word truly show how completely they love him. That is how we know we are living in him. Those who say they live in God should live their lives as Jesus did.
(1 John 2:5–6)

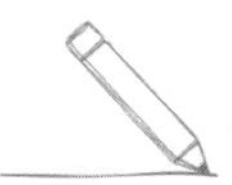

We can easily fall short of showing God's love in our lives. But God calls us to act in obedience to him. For some that will mean stepping into a new way of life, occasionally completely, but often it means small, incremental and gradual changes. Those changes can be painful, but they bring renewal.

Draw a butterfly – a symbol associated with new life. As you do, pray to God about the ways you can be more obedient, and the life that will come on the other side of those changes.

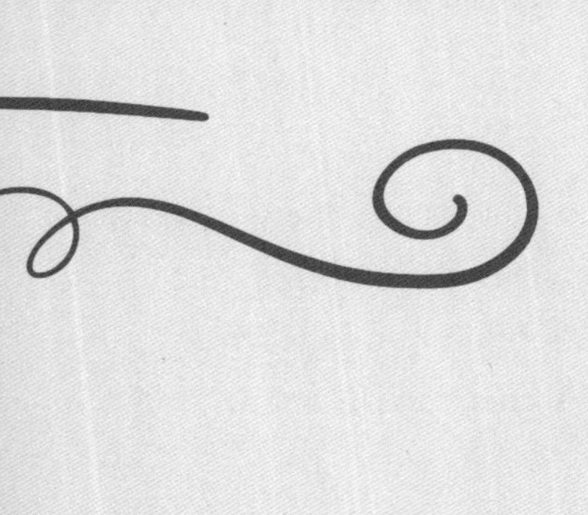

COMMUNITY

We are designed to live in community, but building and maintaining good relationships can be difficult and messy. Let's speak to God about doing it well.

FORGIVENESS

Make allowance for each other's faults, and forgive anyone who offends you. Remember, the Lord forgave you, so you must forgive others.

(Colossians 3:13)

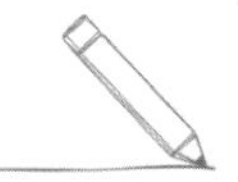

There was an Instagram post I saw recently with a couple in their eighties dancing in the street. The caption said: 'Imagine how many times they've had to forgive each other.' There's something so powerful about forgiveness. We're forgiven daily by God, but from our flawed position it can be hard to do the same.

Draw a bunch of balloons floating away into the sky. As you draw, ask God to bring to mind grievances that need forgiving. Pray that God will give you the strength to let them go and hand them to him.

HARMONY

How good and pleasant it is when God's people live together in unity!
(Psalm 133:1 NIV(UK))

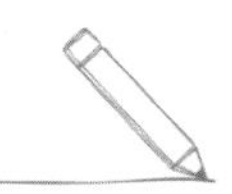

Living well in community is beautiful when done right. That harmony is worth working towards.

Draw musicians playing in an orchestra. As you do, pray to God that your community will be in his perfect harmony, and ask what you can do to contribute to that.

PEACE

Do all that you can to live in peace with everyone.
(Romans 12:18)

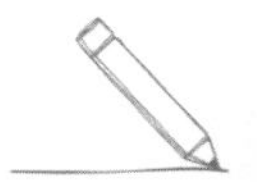

A question I ask myself frequently is, 'Do I want to make a point or do I want to make peace?' We demonstrate Jesus' love when we make allowances for those around us and opt for patience.

Draw an olive branch, a biblical symbol of peace, and ask God how you can bring more peace to your community.

BUILDING EACH OTHER UP

So encourage each other and build each other up, just as you are already doing.
(1 Thessalonians 5:11)

It takes time to build healthy relationships. Each good conversation, kind gesture and thoughtful question is a brick in the wall of a friendship.

Here is a wall. Decorate each of the bricks, one by one, with patterns, designs or anything that springs to mind. As you do, pray to God about the different ways you can continue to build in your relationships.

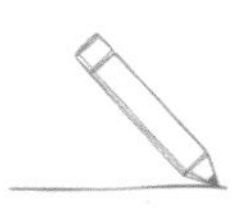

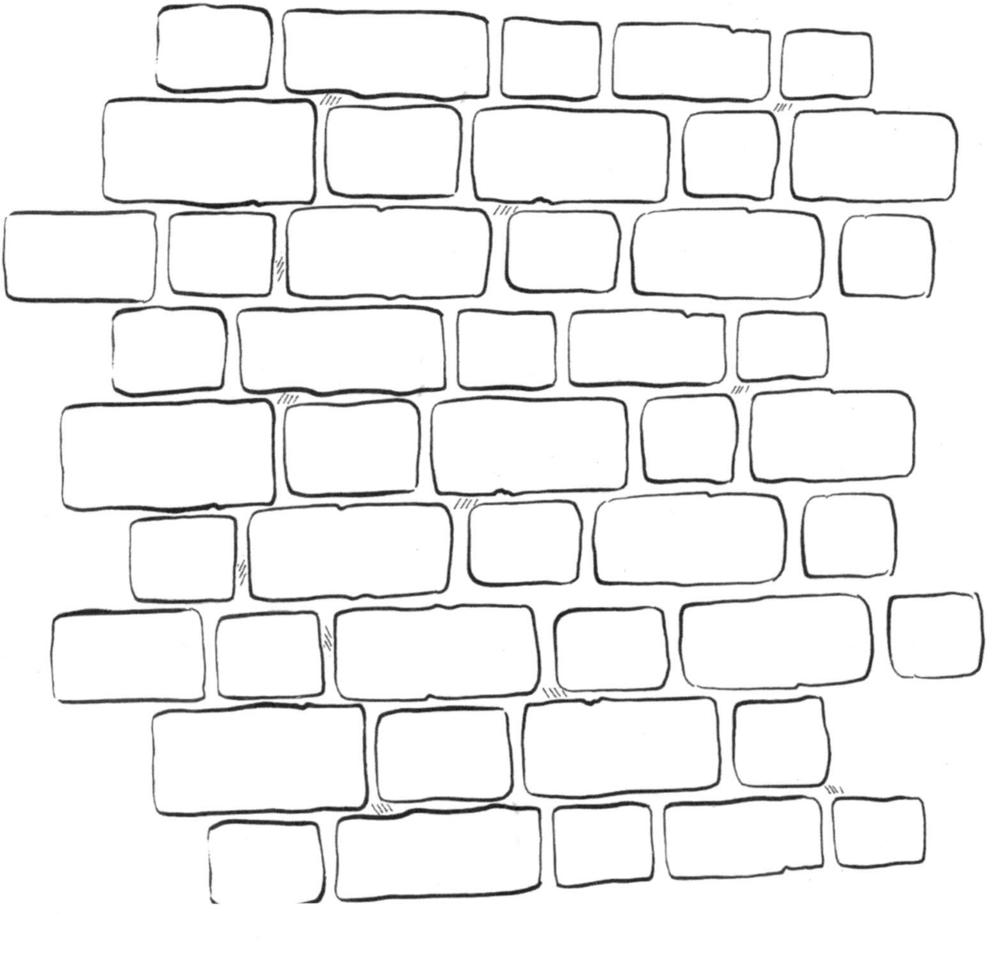

FRIENDSHIP

If one person falls, the other can reach out and help. But someone who falls alone is in real trouble.
(Ecclesiastes 4:10)

We are built to live in community. When times get tough, processing and dealing with a situation on your own only adds to the pain.

Draw a picture of a friend, someone who supports you and stands by you when things are difficult. As you draw, thank God for that friend and for your relationship.

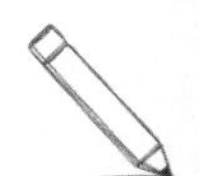

ACCEPTANCE

Therefore, accept each other just as Christ has accepted you so that God will be given glory.

(Romans 15:7)

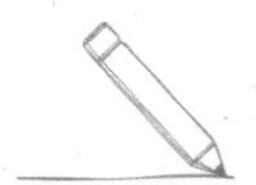

Offering a big welcome to everyone isn't easy. It's unlikely that you'll get on well with absolutely everyone. And yet that's what God has asked us to do – to accept one another as we are.

Draw a table with people sitting around it. As you draw, pray that God would help you to accept everyone and offer them a welcome.

GENEROSITY

But if there are any poor Israelites in your towns when you arrive in the land the LORD your God is giving you, do not be hard-hearted or tightfisted toward them.
(Deuteronomy 15:7)

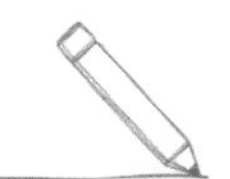

God encourages us to be generous to those who have less than us. That may be by financial giving, but sometimes it's by being generous with something else, like our time or our hospitality.

Draw a pair of hands that are open as opposed to tight-fisted. As you draw, pray that God would show you who you can give to and how best to give to them.

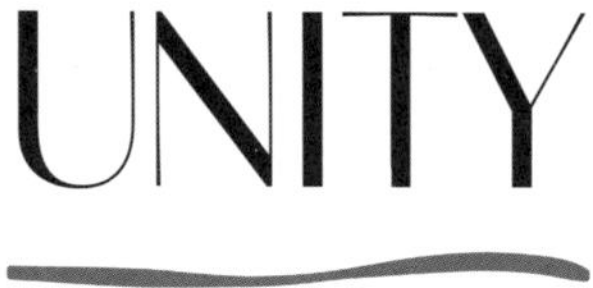

I appeal to you, brothers and sisters, in the name of our Lord Jesus Christ, that all of you agree with one another in what you say and that there be no divisions among you, but that you be perfectly united in mind and thought.
(1 Corinthians 1:10, NIV)

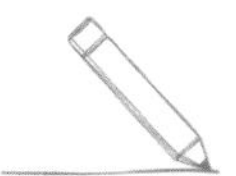

Church community can feel difficult at times. I've got a theory that if you like everyone in your church, you're probably not showing up enough. But our personal preferences aren't important, because each individual is a valuable part.

Draw puzzle pieces that are all slotted together in a sign of unity. As you draw, pray that God would bring your community and/or church together in unity.

IN THE LIGHT

But if we are living in the light, as God is in the light, then we have fellowship with each other, and the blood of Jesus, his Son, cleanses us from all sin.
(1 John 1:7)

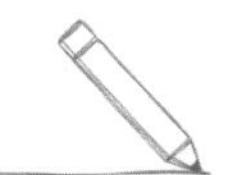

Living in fellowship and 'in the light' isn't as easy as it sounds. Plenty of us keep secrets or feel drawn to things that aren't of God.

Draw a picture of a well-lit path. As you draw, ask God to help you continue to walk in the light, being open and honest with those around you.

PATIENCE

Brothers and sisters, we urge you to warn those who are lazy. Encourage those who are timid. Take tender care of those who are weak. Be patient with everyone.
(1 Thessalonians 5:14)

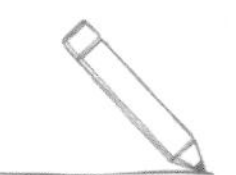

Being patient with everyone is a big ask. People can be annoying and demanding and frustrating. But we are called to walk with them in patience.

Draw a doctor's waiting room – probably the place that promotes the least patience in all of us! As you draw, pray that God would increase your ability to be patient, even with the most difficult people.

SHARING BURDENS

Share each other's burdens, and in this way obey the law of Christ. (Galatians 6:2)

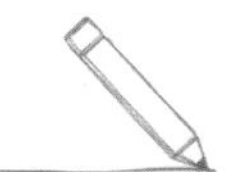

They say that a problem shared is a problem halved – although I don't know who 'they' are, and I think that whether or not this is true really depends on the nature of the problem and who you're sharing it with. But it is true that not feeling alone in your problems can make all the difference.

Draw a Dick-Whittington-style stick-and-hanky combo (the one much loved by fairytale characters running away from home). As you draw, pray that God would help you share your burdens with him and others so the stick and hanky will feel ever lighter.

PRAYER

Confess your sins to each other and pray for each other so that you may be healed. The earnest prayer of a righteous person has great power and produces wonderful results.
(James 5:16)

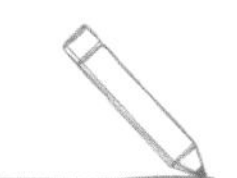

Wisely choosing a couple of people to confide in gives each of us an outlet to bring things we've kept in the darkness into the light. In addiction recovery there's a saying: 'We're only as sick as our secrets.'

Draw a pair of hands together in prayer. As you draw, ask God to show you anything that you need to bring into the light in confession to another person and in prayer to him.

SHARPENING EACH OTHER

As iron sharpens iron, so a friend sharpens a friend.
(Proverbs 27:17)

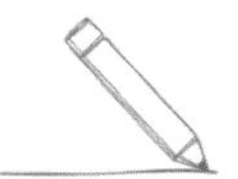

Without trusted friends to challenge and reflect with us, we can go very wrong.

On this page, draw iron sharpening iron. I'll be honest, I would have to Google to know what that looks like. Ironmongery(?) has never been a passion of mine. I may just draw an actual clothes iron and be done with it. But whatever you end up drawing, as you draw, thank God for the friends who sharpen you and the times you have been able to help sharpen those you care about.

LOVE

'This is my commandment: Love each other in the same way I have loved you. There is no greater love than to lay down one's life for one's friends.'
(John 15:12–13)

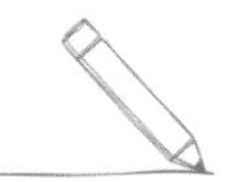

Jesus' love is unrivalled, but we do our best to follow his lead and care for others just as passionately yet gently.

Draw a circle of people joining hands. As you draw, thank God for the way he loves us, and for the amount he sacrificed for that love. Pray that he would ignite a similar passion in you for loving the lost and that he would show you new and innovative ways to demonstrate that love in your life.

A CORD

A person standing alone can be attacked and defeated, but two can stand back-to-back and conquer. Three are even better, for a triple-braided cord is not easily broken.
(Ecclesiastes 4:12)

The strength of friendship, partnership and collaboration is emphasised throughout the Bible. But this example appeals to me as it's so tangible and practical.

Draw a three-stranded cord. It can be like a rope or a plait, or any other interpretation. As you draw, thank God for the strength that comes from community and ask him to strengthen yours.

A FEW PRAYERS TO ROUND OFF

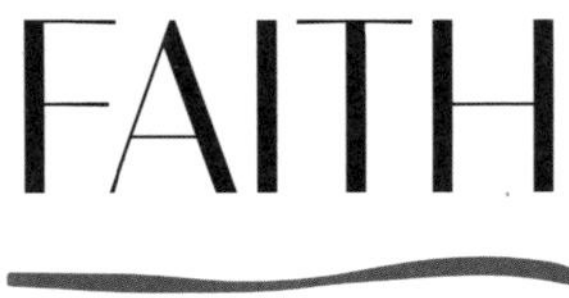

And we know that God causes everything to work together for the good of those who love God and are called according to his purpose for them.
(Romans 8:28)

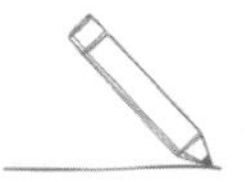

As we come towards the end of the book, let's reflect on God's goodness, particularly when it comes to his care for us. He is steadfast and the safest pair of hands.

Draw something sturdy, something that makes you feel safe just looking at it. Maybe that's a giant mountain or a perfectly built wall. Whatever you choose, as you draw thank God that he is on your side, cheering you on and working for your good.

THE PATH

I know the LORD is always with me. I will not be shaken, for he is right beside me.
(Psalm 16:8)

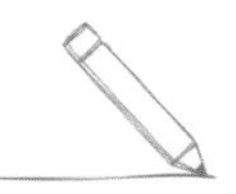

Knowing that God is with you, that he will never leave you nor forsake you, is a calming reassurance. Yet still we can feel anxious and uncertain.

Draw a pair of maracas. As you draw, thank God for his care and support, and pray that you would be able to take peace from it. Pray that, while these maracas may be shaken, you won't be.

REST

Then Jesus said, 'Come to me, all of you who are weary and carry heavy burdens, and I will give you rest.'
(Matthew 11:28)

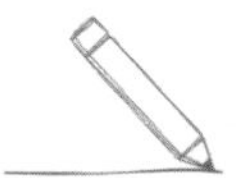

In Jesus we find rest and renewal.

In the space below, draw a bed. As you draw, pray that God would give you good sleep physically, but also good spiritual rest. Pray that he would help you to take time out from work and other commitments when needed and that you would remember to turn to him when you feel weary.

PROTECTION

The LORD is my light and my salvation – so why should I be afraid? The LORD is my fortress, protecting me from danger, so why should I tremble?

(Psalm 27:1–3)

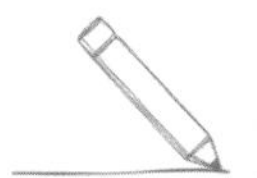

God is our ultimate protector. That doesn't mean hard times won't come. But it does mean that he will give us the strength to face and overcome them.

Draw a picture of a fortress standing tall and strong. As you draw, thank God that you can seek safety in him and that he is your protector.

LISTENING TO HIS VOICE

The LORD directs the steps of the godly. He delights in every detail of their lives.
(Psalm 37:23)

While I was praying about the content of this book (in the conventional non-drawing way), God gave me a picture. I saw myself drawing a picture on a blank sheet of paper. I handed it to God and asked him if he liked it.

Many of us do this. We decide what we're going to draw, make the picture and then hand it to God to ask him to bless it. But I felt God saying that he wants us to present him with the blank page, not the drawing. He wants to decide what to draw with us, not just sign off on the picture once it's done.

So here I've left you some blank pages. Speak to God. Allow him to direct you. Don't present him with the finished article; bring him nothing but a willingness to serve. Ask him what he wants you to draw. As you draw it, ask God to show you if there are other areas of your life where he wants to be included sooner. And from now on, start taking your blank pages to God.

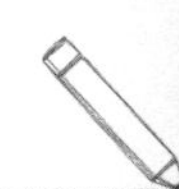

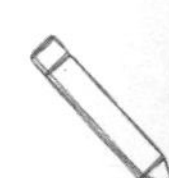